Tears of Joy

A Poetic Journey in the Life of Ms. Joy

Joy Lough

Tears of Joy
A Poetic Journey in the Life of Ms. Joy

© 2012 Anidra (Ms. Joy) Lough

All rights reserved. No part of this book may be resproduced, transmitted or utilized in any form or by any means, electronic or mechanical, including photocopying, recording or by any information storage and retrieval system without written permission of the author.

ISBN 978-0-615-64149-2

Tears of Joy

Acknowledgement

Thank you My Heavenly Father for your mercy and grace. Without you, I know I would not have done anything or been anybody.

Joy Lough

Tears of Joy

Dedications

This book is dedicated to my children, to those who have helped me along my journey in life and to the ones that gave me inspiration. Without you, most of these poems would not exist. ☺

Joy Lough

Tears of Joy

Table of Contents

Section one………Me	11
Intro to Why I Cry	12
Why I Cry	13
Section two……..Life Poems	21
Dear God	22
Love	23
Thank You	24
I Look in Your Eyes	26
Thoughts	30
A Poem for my Mother	31
A Poem for my Father	32
The Perfect Man	34
A day to remember	35
Big Brother	36
Lessons Learned	38
Grandmother Savannah	40
Nature	42
Happiness	43
I am	44
Today	45
First Class	48
Section three……..Love Poems	49
You Need to Know	50
Forgive Me	53
What if?	54
The way you make me feel	56
IF	58
Enough	59

Stop	60
I will not	61
If I could.	62
I have nothing	63
Could it be	64
Rewrite	66
Why can't you see	68
If only you knew	70
Feelings	71
Time	72
Because I love you	73
I do	74
To count my love	75
I'm waiting	76
Tell him	78
He Loves Me	80
Another day	82
Intro to Can you	83
Can you?	84
Section Four……..Not so Love Poems	87
Questions	88
I'm Afraid	89
Pen and Paper	90
Funny	92
No Words	93
Fool	94
Because you love me	96
Tell my heart	98
Emotions	100
Never	103
Make it	104

Tears of Joy

Tell Me	106
Fair Warning	107
Fool Part 2	108
My friend	110
What?	114
I let him go	115
Ending	117
Baby its You	118
About the Author	121

Joy Lough

Tears of Joy

Me

This book is a poetic take of snapshots from moments in my life.

Throughout this book, I will share with you some of my poetry that I have written at different stages in my life. I have divided the book into three sections (the stages). The sections include: Life poems, Love poems and Not So Love Poems. It is my hope that you enjoy reading what I have written. It is also a hope that at least a few of the poems (if not all of them) you will be able to relate to and share in the emotion that I am/was feeling at that particular moment in life.

It is now time to experience…..

TEARS OF JOY!!!!

Joy Lough

Section one

The first poem is entitled "Why I Cry". I have chosen this poem as the first poem for several reasons. First, the name of the book is Tears of Joy. I would like for you to keep in mind that my nickname is Joy as well as the feeling of joy. So, the title of the book itself is a play on words but the first poem is an introduction and the first look into who I am – the first steps in this journey of experiencing "Tears of Joy". Second, I wrote this poem at a point in my life when I was wondering what life is/was…. What my purpose in life is/was… and at that time, I couldn't understand much of anything. I was filled with so many emotions. I have, of course, now built a stronger relationship with GOD. But there was once a time when all I did was **<u>CRY!</u>**

I hope you enjoy!!

Tears of Joy

Why I cry…

This poem is about me
My name is Joy
And you would think
With a name like Joy
I would be happy
But I'm not…

You see I have a son
A really smart kid
And oh how I love him
He is my heart…
Last night he asked me why his daddy
Don't love him
And that broke my heart
What could I say?
But baby that's not true
Your daddy does love you
And I do too
And I gave him a great big hug
But inside I cried
Because I know I lied
I lied because my son is 9
And his daddy has only called
3 times
His entire life
And he has only seen him maybe once or twice
And I know it wasn't right
But you see

Joy Lough

His dad is mad at me
He says the one time the condom
Broke
Wasn't the one time that formed his seed
He said it couldn't be

So when the time came to take the test
And put all his doubt to rest
He decided not to show up
He said he didn't need to
He already had his family
And he didn't want to include mine
You see my 9 year old son has a brother
Whose age also is 9

You see…
I do this poetry thing
And sometimes I sing
I like to write and sing
To express my feelings
And once in a while I dream a dream
You know that special dream you dream
Of what you want to be
When you grow up
And I have had plenty of opportunity
To make my dream a reality
But somehow it doesn't seem that destiny
Wants the same for me

Tears of Joy

You see… I met a man
That I thought was a friend
And then one night I woke up
With him on top of me
And I didn't realize or want to accept
What had happened to me
So I didn't tell anyone because
Who would believe me?
I was in denial and I blamed myself
So I tried to keep it all a secret
But now the whole world knows
The secret I couldn't keep
The whole world knows
Because now… she is 3 years old

You see…
I cry because
I am mommy and daddy
And I work
And go to school
And I got this other gig I try to do
That really makes me happy…
But sometimes the burden and stress of life
Gets the best of me
And it's hard to get out of bed
When you don't sleep at night
And that's why I cry

Joy Lough

Sometimes I wonder…With a name like Joy
Where is the joy in my life?
Now don't get me wrong
I do love my children
But why can't I be someone's wife?
Why can't I be in love?
Why can't I find him?
Why won't he find me?
I am now 30 years old
How old do I need to be?

And yes, I have been married before
But that is just a door
I choose to keep closed
You see… he didn't really love me
He would rather beat me
Night after night
And so - yes I cry

I cry because I am an only child
And I have no one to talk to
And I don't blame my father or my mother
But why can't they just LIKE each other?
Why can't we just sit down for Sunday Dinner?
And share each others stories
I wouldn't mind
If for just one time
The past could be left behind
And we could just be
A FAMILY!!

Tears of Joy

You see… I cry because I am scared
I really want to be there
When my children grow up
But look at this world
Look at the hatred
Look at the deceit
And Lord knows I don't want my
Little girl to meet
The kind of guys…that I did
The kind whose goal was to make you cry
The kind who beat out of you all your pride
The kind that keeps you from your dreams
The kind that promises you the world
And then tells you on his knees
That he loves you
And that he cares
And that when the baby comes
He is going to be there
He is going to protect you
He is gonna comfort you
And he only wants the best for you
And he will do all that he has to do
Whatever he has to
When all the while he knows he's lied
That's why I cry

Joy Lough

I cry because children learn from what they see
And what about my son?
He hasn't seen
What a real man looks like
Please…
I haven't seen one
He hasn't seen him because
I haven't met him
So I can't introduce him
To someones who is not there…
I can only tell him
And I can try to show him
And I can only hope that he doesn't learn
From the TV
Or from places that I can't be
Like school
Or practice
Or at a friend's house
You see…
I teach my son what's good
And to do what's right
But for my son
I am afraid
And…That's why I cry

I know that we all have our trials
That we go through
We have to go through them
In order to grow
And had I not written this poem
You would have never known

Tears of Joy

What it is that I go through
And why I feel the way I do
You see outside I smile
But inside I cry!

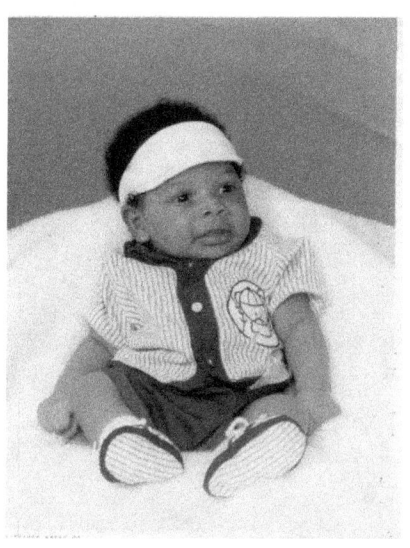

Joy Lough

Tears of Joy

Life poems…

The next set of poems are what I like to call life poems.

Sometimes life can make you wanna scream, cry, boast, brag, wonder and just be thankful.

My Prayer is that you enjoy reading these snapshots!

Joy Lough

Dear God

Thank you!

Thank you for my past
Present and
Future
Thank you for life
Thank you for the rain
Thank you for all the trials
Thank you for the pain
Thank you for all the learned lessons
Thank you for the many blessings
Thank you for Wisdom and Understanding
Thank you for peace
Love
Forgiveness
Happiness
Thank you for being a GOD
I can call at any time
Day or night
And when I wanted to give up
You gave me strength to continue to fight
And even when I strayed
You had MY child to
Pray
For me
And even when I didn't deserve it
You still loved me
You have been my father
And my mother
My best friend
The only one
I can truly depend
On

Thank you!

Tears of Joy

Love

I love who?
I love the one who did
The one who kept me from harm
That one that held me close in his arms
The one that gave me protection
The one who gave me direction
The one who took the pain and doubt away
The one who saw my faults and loved me any way

I love who?
I love the one who is doing
The one who is doing wonderful things in my life
Right here and now
The one who in spite of it all finds a way
Some way some how
The one who showers me with his love
Every day
He not only tells me but he shows me he loves me
In so many different ways
The one who when I am down picks me up
The one the only one I can fully and truly trust

I love who?
I love the one who will do
The one who will always be my best friend
The one who promised me he would be there till the end
And Guess what?
I believe him
He's proved himself time and time again
The one who I know will carry me when I am weak
The one who inspires my words when I speak
The one who gives me courage gives me strength
The one the only one I want to spend my life with
The one who always remains faithful and true
My Heavenly Father…I love you!

Joy Lough

Thank you - A poem for the men in my life

To the ones who left my children fatherless

Because you were less

Of a man

I understand

Now

That things don't always go the way they are planned

I planned to be married one time

With one baby daddy

Through richer or poorer

Sickness and health

Till death do us part

But my soul

My heart

Would not allow me to play the part

Of a punching bag

Or play second in your life

In order to be your wife

You made me wiser and stronger

You made me see

What life can be

Without you

So – thank you………

To the ones that broke my heart

Shattered my dreams

Belittled my accomplishments

And were just plain MEAN

If it were not for you

I could not have seen

How to believe in myself

Tears of Joy

And believe in my dreams too
Like getting my bachelors, masters and now
Doctorate
And I did it all without you
So thank you……
To the ones that cheated on me
Thanks for the pain
Without it
I wouldn't be the same
You made me see
The beauty in me
And most of all
You allowed me to be free
From you
So thank you
This is not a hate poem
And no it doesn't mean that I resent you
I truly do thank you
You have made me who I am
And who I will continue to be
You opened my eyes
To so many possibilities
And I know that inevitably
I had to go through
All you put me through
And for that
From the bottom of my heart
I say thank you

Joy Lough

I look in your eyes
A poem for my children……

My son
I look into your eyes and see so much disappointment and need
and wanting to be
Loved… but not by me…
By your daddy
I see your pain when you watch television and the little boy is
playing catch with his father –
You want that to be you
And I do too
But that's just not our reality
I see your frustration when you have made a huge
accomplishment like good grades or a winning touchdown and he
wasn't there
You keep asking yourself
Why doesn't he just pick up the phone?
To just say hello
Is it really that hard to show that you care?
Knowing the statistics say the odds are against you
That you won't succeed
In what you aspire to be
Because you are a black male
But does it really mean you are destined to fail?
Hell NO!.... And you Remember that!
I see your anxiety because you don't know how to express your
feelings and you don't realize that this is the hand that you were
dealt
And
You need to play this hand
The best you can...
And always understand
That I still love you in spite of it all
I will catch you when you fall
I will be there to dry your tears
Try my best to chase your fears
Away
Just stay

Tears of Joy

Focused on things that are good
Things that are right
And remember that every night
When you lay down to go to bed
Be thankful for the day you had
Ask GOD to continue with you
And to help you do what you need to do
To be a better you
And remember that what I always want to see
Is the best you that you can be!
When I look into your eyes!

When I look into your eyes
Mirakel…my daughter
I look into your eyes
And I know you wonder why
I have even written this poem to you
It's so that you know
That in time you must grow
From being my little baby
To a beautiful young lady
You must know that friends are not always your friends
If they can't stick it out till the end
And that when a boy breaks your heart
It's all a part
Of growing up
Learn from the experiences
Gain wisdom each day
And in every way
That you can
I look in your eyes and I see a beauty
Not just physical but so much more
You care for others so deep
And what GOD has in store
For you

Joy Lough

Words cannot express
I look in your eyes and I see a 9 year old
Trying to grow up faster than she needs to
Stop! and enjoy this journey
And be prepared for where it will lead you
And trust your heart – let it guide you
I look in your eyes and I want you to know
That no matter how far apart we may grow
That I will love you more than you can ever know
And that I believe in you
And how you will touch every life you meet
Keep your inner beauty
And always stay sweet
I look at you and I see a great destiny!

My Children….
When I look into your eyes!

Tears of Joy

Joy Lough

Thoughts - A poem for the child I lost……

Thoughts of you fill my head everyday

You were my life – my miracle

I awake to the morning sun – I think of you

Children playing in the park - I think of you

The thought that when I look at my pillow

I see nothing

It could be you instead

If I had it all to do again

I wouldn't

Every day I live with pain

Heart aching pain such that I cry an ocean full of tears

Not a day goes by that I see another child and I don't think of you

How your smile would be …

Your laughter…Your eyes… Your hair

Your nose… Your ears

Now I will never know……

Moonlight and stars – I think of you

I could be giving you a bath

Putting on your pj's

Reading you a bedtime story

Kissing you on your cheek

Tucking you in at night

Saying I love you…

I just want you to know

That I miss you

Even though I never knew you

And I often wonder

Why have I lost you?

Tears of Joy

A poem for my Mother

When I look at you

I see pure beauty

Nothing less

When I see all the things you go through

And put up with in just one given day

I feel proud

When I think of all that you have accomplished in your life and in

The lives of others

I feel joy

When I watch you

I see the image of a person I hope someday to grow up and be

I stand up MOM

Because I love you

I STAND UP!

Joy Lough

A poem for my Father

A little girl needs her father
A grown woman does too
I really wish our relationship was different
I wish I had the chance to get to know you

As a child I needed to know how to love and not lust
And when giving myself to him
I must
First trust
And believe in myself
And just be
Sure that he was worth me
You see that's what I needed….
From you
I needed to know when to just "like"
A little girl needs to know how to win when she fights
She needs to know when to let go
And when to keep go –ing
To pursue her dreams
I wish just one time you heard me sing
I wish you had a connection with your grandchildren
I wish you were there when
My son played football,
Or when my daughter danced
I wish they knew you
I wish you would have given them the chance
That I didn't have

You see since you weren't there
I didn't have anyone to show me
Or tell me
Or guide me
So Lucky me
Or maybe just dummy me
I found someone just like you
Someone who ran from his responsibilities
And now my children feel exactly like I do

Tears of Joy

Wondering how it would have been different
Wondering if daddy even cares
Wondering if it is something that they did
The reason he is not there
You see no birthday card or Christmas card or phone call
Really scars a child – it leaves a huge void
And even as an adult sometimes I get extremely
Annoyed

Because I am not sure if I can heal
And I'm not really sure what to feel
Or even how to feel
For you

I know that life doesn't always go as planned
And even with your continued absence
I pray for understanding
And I know that you are still my father
And I must love you
Because God asked me to
And because it's the right thing to do
But please know that I really did miss you
Talent shows
Games
Multiple degrees
You were a no show
With all the accomplishments
The desire was still there
And made me want YOU there
Even more

But before my life has come to an end
I just want you to know…And the whole world too
That I forgive you!
And most of all
Inspite of it all
DADDY, I DO LOVE YOU!

The Perfect Man

My daughter asked me today
Who was my perfect "ideal" man?
I paused for a moment
And then I said…

My perfect man
Would allow me to be me
He would nurture my needs
He would want to build with me
He would be understanding
And not controlling

He wouldn't need a lot of money
But can't be afraid to work
Because I know that if he is trying
Then WE can make it work

I want him to love me
Genuinely
He can't be superficial
He needs to be an original
Don't come to me with reused pick up lines
And if he is not a man - Don't be wasting my time

We need to be able to talk to each other
Communicate with one another
We have to LIKE each other
He needs to be there through thick and thin
Of course, I will do the same
And when it really matters
He needs to know to call the right name
He needs to be faithful
Supportive and honest
He needs to be true
But most of all he has to be able to love you
As much as I do!

A Day to Remember

I was twelve years old
Just beginning life with so much to look forward to
And now he was gone
I knew him not as well as I wanted but well enough to remember
My grandfather
He was an intelligent man
Humorous
And
I could talk to him about anything
He was very understanding
An ideal grandfather
His last words to me were
Baby remember I love you
I know you will make me proud
Take care and be a good girl
Trying to think of happy thoughts
I knew he had led a good life and
He was going to a better place
I stood there with my last farewell
Twelve years old

Big Brother

I wish we had a chance to meet
It would have been nice to have you be
In my life
To teach me about boys
And protect me from them too
But God had a different plan
You were gone before I could meet you
It really sucked being an only child
Contrary to what others may say
Growing up would have been awesome
To have someone to play
With
I know you would have been there
When my first love broke my heart
When he made me cry
I know you would have had my back
When I told those little white lies
I could have used your guidance
In many of the decisions I made
I know you would have passed on your knowledge
And wisdom and gave
Me a wonderful role model
To look up to
I hear you were very smart
And from the pictures very handsome too
I know mom really misses you
Every once in a while
She talks about you
And what you two used to do
Together
By the way… I had a son
And named him after you
It would have been great to
Have you in his life too

Tears of Joy

I have to go now…
Take care and hope we can meet someday
I know you are watching down from heaven
I know you hear me when I pray
You are one of my angels God sent to guide me
Watch over me
Help me to see things through
I thank God for your memory
I thank God for you
What I feel for you is like no other
And in the end you will always be
My Big Brother

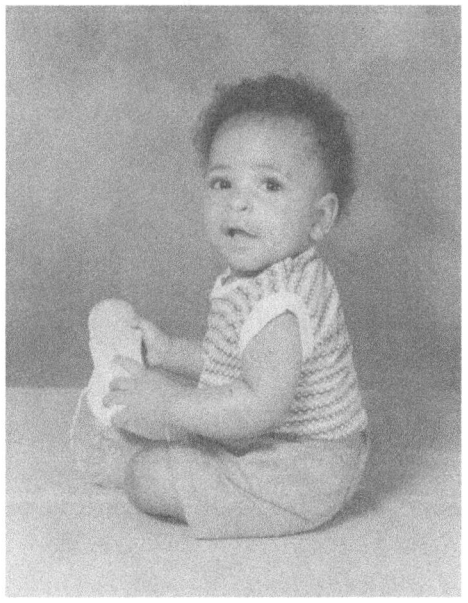

My brother died before I was even born - all I have are a few pictures of him and the stories that other family members tell! This one is dedicated to you – My Big Brother!

Lessons Learned

I have learned that every day no matter what
The sun will come up

I have learned its ok to love him with all your heart
As long as he loves in return
Don't be blinded or fooled by lust
That is the first lesson learned

I have learned that you can't make him change his mind
He will do what he wants to
And No matter how hard you may try
You will be wasting time if his heart doesn't belong to you

I have learned its best to be told a painful truth
Than to be told a glorious lie
Because with the truth you can learn to let go
But with the lie - it can ruin your life

I have learned that people will do
What they want to do
Even if they know
They will hurt you

I have learned not to trust in MAN too much
They will surely one day let you down
I have learned that you will surely get more wrinkles than you desire
If you continue to keep on that frown

I have learned that pouting doesn make it better
And holding on to anger can't make you forget him
When in the end what you need to focus on
Is loving the person within

I have learned to watch what you do and what you say
And that you are responsible for you at the end of the day

Tears of Joy

I have learned sometimes the cards that you are dealt
May feel like a crappy hand
But no matter what you are going through
Remember that God has a plan

I have learned that just because he says he loves you
Doesn't mean he really does
And whatever things may have seemed to be
More than likely it really was

I have learned friends are hard to find and in the end are very few
I have learned in order to find that true friend you have to be one too

I have learned that time doesn't wait for your heart to heal
It continues to move on
And somehow the radio knows exactly what song to play
Every time you turn it on

I have learned even though sometimes you may feel so alone -
like you don't know what to do
It's in that time that you must trust in GOD with all your heart
Because he will see you through

I have learned there are people out there with negative intent
So be careful of where you go and who you spend your time with

I have learned no matter what in your life you have going on
If you listen real close… the Robin is always singing a song

I have learned at the end of the day the sun will set
And yet…
It will rise again…
And give me a new day to learn another lesson.

Grandma Savannah

I miss you
I miss the summers that I spent with you
I miss all the time I spent with you

Amazing how a life can be touched with simple measures
Grandmother what you gave me I will always treasure
You encouraged me
You inspired me
You pushed me to do more
You showed me what life has in store
For me
You accepted me for who I was
You loved me just because
You gave me praise when I did well
And even when I didn't
You told me that fail ing
Was not an option

You were so beautiful
So kind
So gentle

If you were here
I would give you a great big hug
I would tell you I love you
And miss you too
The day you left
I wasn't able to see you go
And there was so much
I needed you to know
But I can wait
Until we meet again
Grandmother –
You will always be my best friend!

My grandmother passed when I was 8 months pregnant with my son. I had a very difficult pregnancy and the doctor advised me not to travel so I never was able to say goodbye and she never got to see her great – grandson. Gramma – I Love you! This one is for you!

Nature – God sent her to me
(Written at 10 years old)

Nature is a best friend
It's always there when you need it to tell your thoughts and dreams
With her many gifts she cares for you in a number of ways
She brings sunshine to brighten up rainy days
And rainy days as an excuse to complain
She gives you animals to become a closer friend
She talks to you with the river and blowing of the trees
And smell of the flowers
She wakes you with sunrise
And sends you to sleep with the moon and stars
She nurses you with the best of goodness
Nature… a friend till the end

Happiness
(I was 9 when I wrote this)

Thinking of happiness
I think of all the wonderful things in life and
How having hardly any of it
Has made me an even happier person
Not having ALL the luxuries in life
Makes me appreciate the things I do have
And makes me happy with what I have
I think of all the other conditions that are worse
That I could be in
And I know and realize that it could be me
Instead of that other person
When I think of happiness I think of peace –world peace for everyone
It's the one thing that we really need and
It would make me an extremely happy person if we had it
Not only me but I'm sure others would be happy too.

The next poem was a poem I wrote for my college applications. In the section that states that you should describe yourself…this is what I said…

I am

I am an ego tripper
I am a superb leader
I pursue the idea of truth and equality
People honor and respect me because of my uniqueness
Proud, though not self centered, I enjoy me
A winner and a hero exist in me

Black is beautiful
I am beautiful
Though beauty is only skin deep
I am beautiful because I care
I am considerate and loving
I want to make life better for others

I am told that a quitter never wins and a winner never quits
So like the hands of time I am persistant in my goals
Though my life has not been all diamonds and pearls
I strive for advancements
I plan to excel and let no one or anything stand in my way

I am phenomenal like a bird
Industrious it cares for itself
Compassionate it provides for its loved ones
A bird was meant to be free
If you cage it you restrict its accomplishments
You hinder its chance to explore
Like a bird I was created
To be free
To love
To sing and
To SOAR

Today

I woke up this morning
And I said no more
No more stressing
No more heart ache
No more pain
I am over the negativity
And the negative people
Around me…

Depression really can get the best of you
If you let it…
And that's just what happened
Yesterday….

I lost it…

I lost my job…
They let me go
And I know why
Because I know
Too much
And I wouldn't lie
And because I was too good
What else could it be?
When the boss tells me
"You making these workers too happy"
Really?
Sounded to me
Like slave mentality
But I had to feed my kids
Give them a place to stay
At least try to show them an Honest way
To make a living
But all that doesn't even matter now
Does it?

Joy Lough

I lost my sanity…
Bills were due
I looked at them
They looked at me
We had a little pity
Party
Invited myself and I
And we cried and cried

I lost my dignity…
I couldn't hold my head high
I didn't know how
I felt like I was lying
To my kids
Going to school will increase
Your chances of employment
But what I really meant
Was…These schools would take all your money
And then take the enjoyment
From you

I lost me…
Didn't want to sing
Didn't want to do any thing
Please don't bother me
Just Let me be

But today…..

Everything is ok
Now I see
The reason why things had to be
The way they were
Now I have the time to do me
And do this poetry thing
And share my story
With others
I have the time to start my own business
Helping others and Encouraging others

Tears of Joy

Now I have time to spend with family
Good quality Time
Time that could not have been spent
Working 50 plus hours per week

Today I took back
My Sanity
My Dignity
My true identity
And from this day forward
I am going to be the best me
I can be
And
It all started
Today

First Class

You see I am on that new stuff
That stuff that will make you say - WOW
I got a new attitude
I'm in a good mood
And the intellect is like POW!

Woke up one day
Made the choice to stay
On this new path
Removed the negativity
Focusing on the possibilities
I sat down and did the math
I know now what is needed
To be to where I want to be
And trust me - this time I'm driving
I refuse to be in the passenger seat

You see…
I'm on a mission
I got this vision
With objectives and goals
The end result will be so epic
So grand
So wonderful
So beautiful

You are welcome to come and join me
But you have to promise me
You will keep an open mind
And that the past will be the past
And it will be left behind
And the mentality should continuously
Be focused on what is vast
You see my name is Ms. Joy
And I am only riding…
First class!

Tears of Joy

Love Poems....

Have you ever been in love so much that sometimes you can't find the words to fully express how you feel? Well, there was once a time when I had the feeling. Well let me be honest, it's been a few times that I have felt that way. Or at least that's what I thought....

The next few poems are the love poems. Some are for the same man and some are for different ones. To the ones who inspired ANY of THESE poems – thank you. These were some really special times in my life.

I hope you like them!

Joy Lough

You need to know

There's something going on here that I just can't explain
Words can't express because my mouth won't form the words
My mouth can't speak the words
It's a mystery
It's like I have stepped into this realm of the unknown
And no I'm not scared because I know you are there
And I'm not sure which way to go
But I do know
That I want you to stay with me
To comfort me
Because… I'm safe with you

It's crazy how every moment I go through thoughts of you
It's like you have even taken over my dreams
It's like I live and breathe YOU
Is there some sort of spell you have on me?
Because it's not like me to do
The things I do
For you

I can't help but wonder if I am living a fantasy
Are you really what I have fathomed you to be?
Can you truly love me
The way I need you to
The way I want you to
The way I love you…..

Tears of Joy

You need to know that I don't just love you

Im in love with you

Sometime I just sit and cry

Tears of joy – sweetie

I never can say good bye

You're stuck with me for the rest of your life

It's like I'm a seed

And you are my sun AND rain

I need you to grow

Are you listening?

Because you really need to know this

You inspire me

You compliment me

You make me – happy

You can't imagine what you do to me

You control me – but in a good way

You fill me

You complete me

You give me a love so beautiful

So pure

You excite me

You touch me and I …mmmmmmmmmmmmmmmmm

You got me feeling like I can't get enough of you

And the things you do….

Can you hear me?

You need to know

There is no one else in my life

Baby I know we can stand this test of time

You see

Joy Lough

I need you

Close to me

Loving me and

I miss you and

Right now

I would give the world away

To have you by my side

You just don't know how much I've prayed

For someone like you

To be in my life

And

Before another day has come and gone

I just had to tell you

Because I think

You need to know

Tears of Joy

Forgive me

If I tell you that you mean the world to me

And you are my everything

And life with you is now complete

It's because I adore you

        If when I awake in the morning beside you

        After all night of making love to you

        The reason why I don't want to leave you

        It's because I treasure you

If I compare you to the man of my dreams

Because heaven has shared this phenomenal being

To me that is how it seems

And it's because I cherish you

        You see the more I am near you

        The more I want to be with you so…

        I think it's time that I told you

        That - yes

        I do love you

So if it seems like I want a little too much time

Baby all I want is to make you mine

I want to spend the rest of my life

With you

Share your name

Be your wife

        It may be too fast to soon

        But love is a flower that is in full bloom

        All my wants

        Are now my needs

        Baby, please

        Forgive me.

Joy Lough

What if?

What if
There was no him and there was no her
Only me and you
Alone in a room
Just us two
And perhaps a bed
Would you?

What if
I brought some candles
Slow jamz and a teddy
Ran a bubble bath
Kissed you from head to toe
Would you let me?

What if
Just for one night
Our bodies could unite
Like a melody and song
And there was no one
Who would know
Tell me…This moment
Would you go?

What if
At the end of this road
All the stories untold
Revealed my destiny
You with me on a journey
Of love and happiness
Would you take me?

Tears of Joy

What if

In my dreams

What I really want and need is YOU

And I asked you to share your world with me

Would you?

Joy Lough

The way you make me feel

It's like winning the lottery
And not having to share the money with anyone
You finally meet that special someone
And you know he is the ONE
And you knew this the very first time you met

It's like waking up on a Saturday morning or even afternoon
Just laying in bed
Watching cartoons
Cuddling and hugging
All day
Because that's what you choose to do
Now what could be more important than making love to you?

It's like meeting for lunch
At your place or mine
For a quickie that leaves the body feeling so sublime
A yearning that you feel deep down inside
Knowing that you are all mine
If I could just press rewind
Give us just a little more time
I……..
Mmmm mmmmm mmmmmm

It's like you are my king
And I am your queen
You have fulfilled my every want and need
I can't explain what you do to me

Tears of Joy

Your love has brought me to my knees
Make me wanna say
"Willl you marry me?"
Sweetie

That's the way you make me feel

Joy Lough

If

If flowers need sunshine and the rain
And love needs both joy and pain
We know this to be true
So if I say I need you
Will you feel the same?

If at night when it gets cold
And all I have is my pillow to hold
And I want you instead my dear
What can I do?
If you are there and I am here?

If day and night I dream of you
Loving me like I love you
If I asked you on my knees
And scream out loud PLEASE
Would you make my dreams come true?

If you could make one wish
And that wish would come true
Would I be what you wished for?
A marriage and baby too?

If I could snap my fingers
And in an instant be next to you
What would you do?
What would you say?
If your love was really true?

Tears of Joy

Enough

I want to
Adore you
Trust you
Care for you
Be with you
Be in love with you
I want to love you all day and all night
In every way possible
But is that
Enough?

Joy Lough

Stop

Stop!

Listen to my cry – a cry of wanting to be loved by you

Look at me but not with your eyes – I want you to see me for who and what I really am

Touch me with more than your hands – I feel the need to be held and I feel I can depend on you

Feel my love – the warmth of my heart is always here and there is a burning inside for you

Taste my love – the sweetness therein it's natural like strawberries

Hold on to my love- its precious and priceless like watching your child take their first steps

Say that you love me and wipe all my tears away

Tears of Joy

I will not

I will not…Be judgemental of you for any reason – I realize that
    Your feelings are fragile but no less important than my own
I will not…Bring up the past – for fear of wiping out the present
I will not…Be jealous of you – I know jealously can desroy a
    Relationship and I don't want to lose you
I will not… Take away your pain – you need it to grow
I will not… Take away your sorrow and grief – you need it to be
    Strong
I will not…Be possessive of you – even though I would like to own
    Your every breath
I will not…Ask for every minute of your time – just every minute of
    Your thoughts
I will not…Only be your woman – but also your friend lover and
    Confidante
I will not…Plan our every moment – surprises are more fun
I will not…Lie to you – even though the truth will hurt you more
I will not…Try to change you – I accept you "as is"
I will not…Have expectations of you – the ones you have of yourself
    Are great enough
I will not…Stop loving you…No Matter what!

Joy Lough

If I could

If I could…I would make your dreams reality

If I could… I would cry all your tears

If I could…I would feel all your fears

If I could…I would tell the whole world how much I need you, want you
    And adore you

If I could…I would give you the world – anything you want because
    You mean that much to me

But I will never stop loving you

Even if I could.

Tears of Joy

I have nothing

I have pictures to look at that capture your smile but they do not talk to me

I have the teddy bear that you gave me and I hold it all the time but it cannot hold me back

I have all the letters you have written to me with love but they cannot love me

I have a song in my heart that I want to sing but you are not here to listen

I have all the memories that we have shared but I am now making memories without you

I have all these things… but I really have nothing without you!

Joy Lough

Could it be…..?

Could it be you are the one?
The one to make my dreams come true?
Could it be that my search is finally over
And from now till the end it will be me and you?

Could it be that destiny
This time sent true love
After all the prayers I have prayed
To the stars and the heavens above?

Could it be that when I awake
You will still be here
Right by my side
Saying that you love me
And it's gonna be alright?

See I told myself when I give my love this time
Im gonna give it all I got and then a little more
Could it be that you were the one that heard my cry and
That love has finally opened its door?
Could it be you are my happy ending
My perfect paradise
Here to kiss away all the pain
And tell me love is here to stay this time?

I am told that some dreams can come true
Could it be I found my dream when I found you?

Tears of Joy

I really can't explain what it is that I feel for you
But im sure in time what will be will be
So if it's not love
Tell me
What could it be???

Joy Lough

REWRITE

Our love story….
We meet we talk
We greet
We plan to walk
Thru whatever comes our way

You so fine
Me so beau- ti- ful
That's what you said
That's what I say

Misunderstandings
High expectations
Low self esteem
Yet wonderful relations
Mindblowing
Breath taking
Steamy hot
Awesome lovemaking

Unnecessary Irritation
Anger fear
Exasperation/ frustration
Voices loud
Hands raised
With no apologies
And then you leave……
Resentment
Unhappiness
And even through it all
I still miss…….You

Let's rewrite our love
This time let's make it true
Let's have a happy ending
Let's start with "I DO"
Make you a more gentle and kind man

Tears of Joy

Make me more understanding
Let's keep the passion
And lovemaking
No more disappointments
No more heart breaking
No more tears
No more fears
Instead of days
Let's make it years
Let's keep it real
Let's keep it new
Let's keep it
Just us two
This time will be
Everything we want and need
This time will be
Our future
Our destiny
This time we talk
This time we listen
And pray to the Father above
He will guide us
He will keep us
He will help us
Rewrite our love

Joy Lough

Why can't you see?

I'm not going NOWHERE
Unless you want me to
Do you?
I hope not
Cause if you did
I would just drop
Dead
That's just how I feel
Baby this is real
This feeling I feel
I can't explain
All I know is that
It's no game
I want you to stay with me
Share my world
Share my life
Grow together
We are so right
For each other
Why can't you see that
I'm here waiting patiently
Beacause I know you are my destiny
We were made to be…
Together
Everything that happened
Before I met you
Was preparing me to
Get to you
So no…I won't just let you go

Tears of Joy

I won't just walk away
Today just might be the day
That you really need someone
And I want to be that someone
I want you to see
It's not all about me
It's about us
And right now it's about
Trust!!!!
You have my heart
My mind body and soul
And I need to know
That you feel the same…..
You see…I think of you
I dream about you
Making love to you
I imagine what its like
Waking up in your arms daily
Feeling your warm touch
Your strong hands
Just maybe
One day you will see….
Don't be afraid
I'm not hear to hurt you
All I want to do is love you
And I know you love me too
Your eyes tell me you do
Everytime you look at me
Why can't you see?

Joy Lough

If you only knew

If you only knew

I think about you everyday and dream about you at night

If you only knew

How happy I would be if you told me we would spend eternity together

If you only knew

Driving in my car I see you next to me I feel you holding my hand… but you are not there

If you only knew

Every night I turn over in my sleep and hold on tight to my pillow – wishing it were you instead

If you only knew

I feel that only time can bring us together – I need you here with me

If you only knew

My life continues to be a song unsung, a story untold, a dream deferred without you

If you only knew

How many ways I love you

Tears of Joy

Feelings

My feelings are like a priceless gem
That could never be replaced
My thoughts of you are like a perfect summer day
My love for you is like a piece of gold
My heart is like a flower – gentle and as fragile as can be
This is how I feel for you
My love for you will always be true
My feelings for you will never change
My thoughts of you will always be the same
I pray we will never grow apart
Because in your hands
You are holding my heart

Joy Lough

Time

Time brought us together
We've had good times
We've had bad times
There have been joyous times
And times of sorrow that we have shared
With time I have learned to
Respect you
And need you
Trust you
Believe in you
And adore you
And I will love you
Until the end of time

Tears of Joy

Because I love you

Since the day we first met I knew you were the one for me.

I promise to give you everything that I have for you are everything to me.

When we are apart I sure do miss you.

When I am with you I am the happiest person in the world.

I hope you need and want me the way I do you.

I need to be with you always.

I want to be with you forever and a day and

I promise to cherish, respect and trust you for who you are

Because I love you!

Joy Lough

I Do (My Vows of Love)

As we take each others hand and promise to faithfully walk down this road of life together I want you to know that I love you with all my mind body and soul with all that I have

Spending time wih you is how I want to spend the rest of my life

I am sure we will have our share of good and bad times as with any relationship - but I want to have all my good and bad times with no one else but you

I will give you my life if you asked me to

All I ask is that you give all that you have to give

Faithfully

Cheerfully and

Willingly

With respect and

I promise to do the same

For always and forever

I DO

Tears of Joy

To count my love

To count my love would be like counting drops of water in the ocean - you will be counting forever

To see my love would be like standing on top of a mountain top looking at the world endlessly – no starting point – no ending point

To smell my love would be like sitting in a field of roses – the smell would give tranquility peace and harmony

To feel my love would be like a warm summer day lying under an oak tree with a cool breeze blowing – you feel it through your soul

To touch my love would be like lying on a cloud – here on earth…it's the softest place on earth

But I will give it all up to be with you

Can't you see…I just want to be counted?

Joy Lough

Im waiting

To hear your voice
To see your face
To feel the warmth
Of your embrace
Will you be
The man I need?
The one I will love
For eternity?
Patience is a virtue
Yes this is true
But how much longer
Must I wait to hear
From you
If tonight I get no call
If tonight I get no show
Then tonight will be the night
That I will definitely know
If you are for real
Or just playing games and
If what you want and
What I want are both the same
Will you be the one?
Can you be the one?
For me?
For tonight is the night that
We will surely see
Just wanna let you know
I aint mad at you

Tears of Joy

If there is nothing there
I still have love for you
And I will be here

Waiting for you

Joy Lough

Tell Him

Tell him… I love him
Even though we can't be
You see –
He just doesn't understand me
He doesn't understand my needs
He can only be
What he was taught to be
And the person that he is - isn't right for me
Don't get me wrong
He is beautiful – oh so beautiful
And the moments we shared were oh so wonderful
His smile so warm
His heart so pure
His touch so gentle
His love so true
If only he knew what he meant to me
If only he could vision what it is that I see
If only he could feel and understand the depth of ME
And what we could together one day be
I wanted to be everything he ever needed
But he wouldn't let me
He didn't know how
And even though he tried to please me
It just was somehow
Not enough to make this flower grow
And even though it hurts my heart
I just had to let him go

Tears of Joy

And yes I still love him
And yes I still care
And though we can't be together I will always be there
And maybe just maybe one day he will see
That a woman needs a man who is willing to be...

Her knight in shining amour
Her homey, lover and friend
Someone she can trust, confide and believe in
Through ups and downs and through thick and thin
Until this mortal life comes to an end

I hope that destiny has another plan for me
And I pray to God that the next time will be
Whatever it is that God has intended for me

So another journey in my life - I must now begin
But please before I go
Tell him I love him!

Joy Lough

He Loves me

He loves me

He loves me not

He loves me

He loves me not only in mind but in body and soul

He loves me

He loves me from my head to my toes

He loves me

He makes me feel so lovely – so sexy

He loves me

He loves me so deeply and completely

He loves me

He loves me not only for who I am but for what I am - I am a strong black woman who also loves her man mind body and soul

We got that kind of love that makes you wanna loose control

The kind of love that I just don't want to let go

That kind of love that's you know – unbreakable

He loves me

He walks beside me standing tall

He loves me

In everything he does he gives his all

He loves me

You see these arms and these hands

They hold me tight

It's these arms and these hands that keep me safe at night

He loves me

He not only gives me what I want but also what I need

Tears of Joy

When I am scared he calms my fears and
When I cry he dries all my tears
He loves me
All I have to do is ask and I shall receive
Be it money or diamonds or pearls
He loves me...
You see my man would give me the world
Now you may ask yourself – How can this be?
My answer to you is because he loves me

Joy Lough

Another day

It used to be...
Another day of loneliness
Another day of nothing but stress on top of stress
Another day of how am I going to make it?
Another day of why even try to make it?
Another day of saying please loose my number – don't call me anymore
Another day of what could I have possibly thought I needed you for?
Another day of... for him doing all that I can
And him NEVER recognizing the queen that I am
And because he was not the one chosen for me
Another day of deferring my dreams
Another day of I will never trust another man again
Another day because ALL MEN are trifling!
Now it's...
Another day of I can't wait to see you
Another day of thoughts and visions of you
Another day of smiles and laughter
Another day of lovemaking and the morning after
Another day of happiness and belonging
Another day of needing and wanting
Another day of can this really be true?
Another day of how deep the love is I feel for you
Another day of newness and originality
Another day of fullness and compatibility
Another day of not having to wonder if it's only me
Another day of feeling so complete
You see...
Every day I pray that I live to see
Another day for you and me

Tears of Joy

Have you ever just wanted to find that special person in your life? The one that makes all your dreams come true. Well, the next poem is about my desire to find that special person. I have recited it in a few open mics and I have actually recited to a few men that have come across in my life. The funny things is most of the guys would answer "YES". I am like ….really? That's all I get? I laugh hysterically often when I look back and remember some of the responses that I have received. There was once a guy that came back with a response via poem. If you are reading this… you know who you are. Thank you for your originality.

To the person that inspired me to write it because you were definitely everything that was the opposite of what I wanted - thank you also.

Joy Lough

Can you?

I dream of a place filled with tranqulity
Roses and flowers in bloom
Watching the sunrise and sunset
Making love at high noon
No worries or cares
Just me and you
You're all I want
My dream come true
A perfect moment
What can I say?
Can you take me there?
Can you take me away?

I need you to be beside me
I need you close to me
Love me guide me
I need you to be the first person I see in the morning
The last face I see at night
And oh in between as our bodies take flight
You feel warmth within your soul
As you loose total control
All your fantasies
Become reality
But I have to ask….
Can you need me?

To hear your voice and feel your touch
That's what I need and want so much

Tears of Joy

Stay with me beyond the end
Be my lover and also my friend
My angel show me the way
To your heart so that we may
Last for all eternity
Question….
Can you love me?

Toes up high
Feet presssing against the sky
A gentle kiss from head to toe
Not a spot to miss and don't let go
Dip and sway
Move with me in every way
Every night and every day
Can you love me that way?

If I say "I do"
Can you say that too?
If all of me wants all of you
Can you be that love so true?
If all my trust is in your hands
Can you be that type of man
That will be faithful and understand
That love is present right here and now
Though it wasn't planned
Will you somehow
Believe
And say "Yes, I can"
Can you?

Joy Lough

Tears of Joy

Hate poems....

The following poems are definitely not love poems. You could say they are hate poems or just not so in love poems....

Call them HHHMMM poems—

They could be called maybe? poems....

Make you wonder poems...

Think about it again poems...

Read it one more time poems....

I hope they allow you to reminisce, relate, appreciate, laugh and understand me more....

Enjoy!

Questions…

Tell me…
Do you know how to catch a falling star?
Can you really mend a broken heart?
Do dreams you believe in really come true?
Because I believe in dreams like I believed in you…
Will I ever get over you?
Will my grey skies turn back blue?
Why is my heart filled with regret?
Is there really a way to forgive and forget?

Naïve was I to think you even cared
I believed you when you told me you would always be there
So tell me where's the love you promised me?
Where has it gone?
And why?

Was the world I lived in – just a fantasy?
Believe it or not…
A part of me wants to go back to living that lie.

For you to answer these questions
Is what I request
Please be honest
And in the answers give your best

Did you ever love me?
Was anything from you true?
Because if it all was just fiction
Why did you even say I DO?

Tears of Joy

Im afraid

It started out with butterflies

The shine….The smile…The glow

That love that made the universe move

A love that only heaven would know

The lovemaking that brought tears to my eyes

You were the sun and I the moon

I would have never imagined in my wildest dreams

The depth of love you brought me to….

The time when time was on our side

Now it separates us

Leaving me feeling so alone

Keeping me wondering should I trust?

Of course I should

What we have is good

And I know that I have you

To travel with me through this journey of life

At least I think I do…..

Tell me what brought on the change

Was it something I did wrong?

Whats the reason for you treating me this way?

And why don't you return my calls?

Am I so naïve that I can't see

That you have let me go

Where is the you that I once knew

Just 7 days ago?

I try to see the point

But I only see the pain

Why can't YOU SEE?

That

Im afraid

Joy Lough

Pen and paper

What if I didn't have pen and paper
To write
To express how I feel about you
To get me through this night
Don't you know if I saw you right now
I would honestly KILL YOU
And not even think twice about it

        What if I had writer's block right now
        And this pen and paper didn't work
        How can you sleep at night?
        Knowing all the hurt
        You have caused
        What the hell did I do to you?
        I did nothing but love you
        You will never find another love
        So faithful and true
        Don't ever even think you will
        YOU WON'T

                GOD is definitely on your side right now
                For me not to just get in my car
                And drive down there
                Believe me you don't want to see me right now
                And you need to thank GOD for giving me the strength
                Not to just blow up all your shit
                And then go and find that bitch
                That got between us….

Tears of Joy

It's like you didn't even take heed
When I said
That another man would never treat me this way again
How long did you think you could have pulled this off?
Did you think that I would never know?
Did you honestly think that I was so naïve that I would never know?

You need to get on your knees
And thank your lucky stars
Because this pen and paper has actually saved your life
This pen and paper has allowed me to write
Down what I was thinking
Instead of me actually doing what I was thinking
YES, PEN AND PAPER!

Joy Lough

Funny

Funny how things on the outside
Are not what they are on the insde
Funny how my life just keeps repeating itself
Funny the man I love
He just changed his mind
Funny how I keep wasting time
Too much too fast
No one to blame but me
For even thinking it would last
Funny how dreams
Remain dreams
Funny - I believe everything
Happens for a reason
I'm a good woman
A good mother
There is nothing I wouldn't do for that special someone
And I am still waiting
For my time of true happiness
Isn't that funny?

Tears of Joy

No words

I can be alone
By myself
Sometimes I am lonely with you
Something is wrong
How do I love you?
I am happiest when we make love
The music we make is a song of love and joy
I am saddest when you are away
My heart has a missing part
Useless like a broken radio
Like an ice cream cone without the ice cream
My world is complete when I'm with you
Sometimes…..
I feel we will always be together
Though I know we really won't
You are my life
I love to make you happy
I need you holding me
Kissing me
Loving me
Do you….
Then I feel you could care less
Im just another Woman that has been your fool
Living in your world
A fantasy world
And yet I still love you
Why??????

Joy Lough

Fool

Remember when you said you would call – but my phone didn't ring
And when I asked you about it – you said the craziest thing
Happened

Remember when you said you would stop by and I stayed up all night
And when I asked you about it – that conversation turned into a fight

Yes it was a little too fast
A little too soon
But you said you were digging me and I know I was digging you
You said there was nothing in the world you wouldn't do
For me

Its crazy how things just change
Just like your mind did on yesterday….

You see I believed all your lies
And your sorry alibis
Time after time
Because you were mine
My man
And baby we had plans
Don't you remember?

What the hell did you think I was going to say?
When you finally got the nerve to tell me the way
You truly feel
How you never really got over her
How you never stopped loving her

Tears of Joy

How being with me
At least you thought
Would make you forget her
FORGET HER
And
FORGET YOU

Trust and believe
The next will do to you
What you have done to me
Times three

No I do not accept your apology
It's over now and I finally see
That the part of the "fool"
You had me play
But it was what I needed
In order for me to say…….
Goodbye!

Joy Lough

Because You love me…

It don't even matter that you don't call
And you don't return my calls
And it don't even matter that you didn't come home
Last night
Because you love me right?

        And so what I waited on you
        And cooked dinner just for
        The two of us
        And you never even showed up
        Why should I be mad sweety?
        Because you love me right?

                And never mind the fact that I finally found out
                About her
                Yea all that was in the dark
                Has now come to light
                Baby never mind all of that
                Because you love me right?

And it doesn't even make a difference
The fact that she told me that you told her
That you loved her too
C'mon… What kind of fool does she think I am?
You love ME right?

Tears of Joy

And this ring on my hand
It symbolizes us as man and wife
And Nothing else matters baby
Because you love me right?

        So don't take this to heart
        Now that we must part
        See I've taken my turn and played the love game
        And…

                Damn I'm sure gonna miss you
                And what we had
                It's really a shame
                Because I really did love you
                With all that I have inside

        But you really didn't love me
        Right?
        The right way?
        There's nothing else to say
        Because you never loved me anyway….

Joy Lough

Tell my heart

Tell my heart not to love you
Because I really have tried
But it just won't listen to me
It only seems to cry

Tell my heart not to want you
Tell it not to hurt so bad
When I see other lovers kissing
Or even just holding hands

Tell my heart not to think of you
And thoughts of what used to be
Tell it not to take my breath away
Every time I try to breath

Tell my heart to get over you
And let me sleep for just one night
Tell these tears to stop falling
And find a way to just dry

Tell these dreams to go away
They're no longer a possibility
It doesn't matter how much I've prayed
You are not coming back to me

Tell my mind not to wonder
If you even think of me
Truth is – it doesn't really matter
We are no longer a reality

Tears of Joy

So Tell my heart to stop aching
What can possibly be gained?
Its time to just realize
You won't be back again

And even though I still love you
And cannot deny how I feel
Will SOMEONE please tell my heart
To give itself - the time it needs to heal

Joy Lough

EMOTIONS

It's like
Night and day
Dark and light
Left and right
Right and wrong
Weak and strong
You
Make me happy
Make me sad
Make me good
Make me bad
We
Up and down
Here and there
Love and hate
Dreams and nightmares
You
Protect me
Love me
Hold me
Console me
Then you
Neglect me
Hate me
Use me
Abuse me
Can we...
Make this better
Make it right
Make us 3
You, me and baby
Should we
Let it go
Walk away
Or turn around
And try to stay

Tears of Joy

Do you…
Hear my cry
Hear my plea
All I want
Is to be happy
Can we
Talk and not fight
Embrace this new life
Whatever is wrong
Make it right
Make fantasies – reality
Make hopes and dreams-
Possibilities
If it's meant to be
We owe it to ourselves to at least try
Just one more time before we say goodbye
Leave the hurtful past in the past
Erase what was did and said
Start all new
Because through it all
I still love you
And I wanna love you more
Each day
I wanna find the words to help me say
That I
Need you
And want you
I adore you
And cherish you
And I
Want the chance again to
Hold you
Touch you
Kiss you
And make love to you
PLEASE…

Joy Lough

Give that to me
I need you to Be
My refuse
My strength
My peace
My happiness
Will you do that for me?

Tears of Joy

Never

Never again that's what I said
To myself
Never would my physical
Spiritual
Emotional and
Mental
To be taken for granted
So why are you still here?
What's your reasoning?
What is my life -?
A game to you?
I don't think so
You had your ONE chance to
Hurt me
I opened up to you
I believed in you and I trusted you
You will never get another chance
DO YOU HEAR ME?
Never

Joy Lough

Make it

I remember when we 1st met
Your smile and the time we spent
I will never forget it
How you would call just because
I need you to make it like it was

These tears I cry I can't seem to stop
And believe me I am trying
But the pain won't stop
You need to know it's gonna take more
Than occasional kisses
And some occasional time
For the Mrs.
To be all that she can be
For me to realize
For it to finally hit me
That it won't be me
Having your baby
No matter how hard I try
I can't deny
That's what I really want
I feel it's what I need
To be complete
For us to be
A family

Make me happy
Make this better
Make me forget about her

Tears of Joy

Do whatever it takes
To turn these grey skies blue
Make this love new
Do whatever you need to do
To Make me love you
More

Make me grow
Make me trust you
Make me know
That you really love me too
Understand me
Here what I say
Baby please
Make it go away

Joy Lough

Tell me

Tell me where did we go wrong
From where I stood
Everything was good
But it seems from where you stood
you saw the opposite
When I felt there could be no opposite

You made rain out of sunshine
You made tears come from my eyes
Where is the man that I know that
Would start my day off good
like the sunrise?

Im all alone putting the pieces together
But I can't find the piece
That makes you loose interest in me
Think we were meant to be
Like it's our destiny
Do I want you to leave me?
No
But you keep playing with my heart
Whoever thought we'd break a part
Wish I had seen it from the start

Tears of Joy

Fair warning

You need to tell your chic
She is running out of time
Because the things I will do and say
Will totally captivate your mind

Tell her she needs to be careful
Not coming home some nights
Because real soon will be when
Im gonna be with you at night - alright?

Tell her to stop sleeping
On her duties as your mate
Or pretty soon I will be creeping
Cooking and sleeping at your place

You need to tell her
She needs to watch her back
Because I know that you have needs
And fulfilling those needs
That's where Im at

Remind her that you are a king
Intellectual handsome and Strong
And that in me you will find what you need
And I said that with me is where you belong

Tell her I'm giving her fair warning
To appreciate the man she got
And Tell her that I am the one
That will do
Everything she does not

Joy Lough

Fool part 2

It's hard for me to understand
What exactly is going on
I thought we were building something magnificent
Now im wondering where I belong

In times of sorrow – I want to be your shoulder
When you need love – I want to be your lover
If you need a friend I want to be the best
I don't want you to feel the need to turn to another

Now I do know that your life existed before me
And I understand that you are set in your ways
Im not asking you to change for me
Just asking for a little more time from your day

Don't leave me hanging on promises
And please don't lie to me
If you would just open up
You will see that I am all you will ever need

Im waiting here with my open arms
And still you don't receive
So tell me what I need to do
In order for you to believe

I have prayed for someone true
To come into my life
And for whatever reason I met you
And WE planned for me to become your wife

If for some reason your mind has changed
And you have made other plans
Then all I ask is that you let me know
Just tell me where I stand

I know you have a lot on your plate now
And I am really not trying to add on

Tears of Joy

As I have told you before my love
Im here for you to lean on

Now I don't want you to think
Im hanging on to my past
I do want you to realize that I do have both eyes open
And I'm not gonna make the same mistake as I did with the last

You have asked me if you were my man
And I have told you yes
Now I am asking am I your woman?
And tonight I will take whatever answer I get
And if there is no answer
Then I will surely know
Because this is not a hard thing to do
Simply say yes….. or no
Because I want to stand beside you
I want to love you too
But I won't stand her waiting on you to make up your mind
I won't stand here playing the part of the fool.

Joy Lough

My friend

I have a story to tell
And I ask u please
To listen - and help me
U see – I am so confused

I just ended a relationship
With this guy
Who I thought loved me
But finally realized it all
Was a lie
When just a week after the proposal
He so stupid
He Left his phone and
She called and I answered
And
She told me everything

So when I needed someone to talk to
I called my friend
We go back for a short time
And I kinda secretly like him
But I can't tell him

I asked him to come over
And to be my ear
And I really didn't want to talk
 I just wanted someone near
To take away the pain
At least for the moment

Tears of Joy

U know to help me
Get thru it
I just wanted to forget.......

And he was there
I mean -he was there
And he looked so good
And at that moment I wanted
To tell him
But he is my friend

I don't want to loose
His friendship
U see it is extremely dear to me
But there is more to this story…

That night
I was weak and he smelled
So good
I couldn't help but wonder
If I should
Take a chance…
And so I leaned forward
To see if he would respond
Then the next thing I know
He was holding me in his arms
And I got butterflies

I was feeling like
O my goodness!!
What did I do?

Joy Lough

But I can't stop now
Please - I aint no fool
At that moment I wanted him
Desperately...
But he is my friend

Now should I or not?
Yes I should so I do
And I can't stop
Because curiosity
Is getting the best of me
But he's my friend

I'm getting chills down my spine
 My hearts beating really
Fast
Secretly I wanted this all the time
And he has no idea
He kissed me
Gently
Passionately
He made my body FEEL

A pure state of exhaustion
From all the Ecstasy
An experience of
Eternity
But just for a moment
Can this actually be?

Tears of Joy

Now those feelings I felt before
Have just tripled
And now I am wanting more
But he's my friend

I guess I have to wait
Maybe he feels the same
But I'm not gonna say
Anything of what I am feeling before he does
So I will let time pass by
And secretly hide
What I am feeling inside
Because...
He is my friend

What?

You must think I am totally stupid
Do you really believe that I believe
That there is a cupid?

So you think that we are meant to be?
Really?
Hhmmm
Then explain to me what it is that you can do for me?

Let's see ….I have a house – make that two
2 cars and I take care of my 2 kids
My bills are paid on time
Baby …I'm making money all kinds of ways
Even as you read this rhyme
And trust…I got that thing
That handles that other thing too
So tell me why you honestly think
I would possibly NEED you?

Don't get me wrong
It would be nice to have a man
But that equates to me wanting a man
Not needing a man
Do you understand?

There is a difference between the two
All I am saying is that you
Must bring more to the table
Than just a desire to say…I DO

Did you not read the other poems?
Did you not see what I have been through?
You may have looks, body, and money too…
But what else do you have to make me want you?
What?

Tears of Joy

I let him go

There is no more him
I let him go…
because
He had me on this emotional roller coaster
It was like I was the poster
Child of
"Heartache and heart break and
Love and hate and
Ms. Make Many Mistakes and
Baby please, I will do whatever it takes
And
Can you please take
Advantage of me?"
He loved me
Then he loved me not
Who does that?
Really? – WHO DOES THAT?
What he had was emotional constipation
He words were full of manipulation
Didn't give me intellectual conversation
His stories were full of exaggerations
And what I needed was
A separation
From him
Then it hit me
My revelation
What I really needed
In a relation-
Ship
Was mental stimulation
Not physical Aggravation
Or financial frustration
Or even Visual irritation
And during this evaluation
I also realized that
The stipulation
I needed
Was To have determination

Joy Lough

And resist temptation
So that my situation
Would have elevation
You see
I needed to focus on the
Edification and
Dedication
Of me
Because he
Was not giving that to me
And
I can't love him
I won't love him
When he doesn't love me
When he doesn't know if he loves me
When he just doesn't know me
Or when he just doesn't know
So

I let him go

Tears of Joy

I wanted to end on a good note....

This poem is actually a song I wrote for someone very special....

Enjoy!

Joy Lough

Baby it's you!

Baby it's you

You're the only one for me

Like a flower needs the rain

It's you that I need

Come whatever may

I want you to stay

Make all my dreams come true

Baby it's you…

Never felt this way before

The things you do to me

You have brought my heart so much joy

You make me…. happy

When nights are long and cold

You are there to keep me warm

When I needed a friend

You have been my shoulder to cry on

All I do is think of you

You are always on my mind

In each and every single way

I promise to keep you satisfied

If ever a love was meant to be

Baby it's you and me

I know I can make you happy

Baby, My love for you is true

I'm a good woman lover and friend

Let me prove it to you

Baby it's you I want to share my life with

Only you can make it right

Tears of Joy

Through all my good and bad times
I want you right by my side
If ever a love was meant to be
Baby it's you and me
I don't want another love
You are the man of my dreams
Come hold me in your arms
Make my world complete
This feeling is so strong
I want the world to see
If ever a love was meant to be
Baby it's you and me!

Joy Lough

Thank you for purchasing my book.

Tears of Joy

About the author:

Joy Lough received her Bachelor of Science Degree in Business Management with a concentration on Human Resource Management from Guilford College in Greensboro, NC. She received her Executive Master of Business Administration from Colorado Technical University in Colorado Springs, CO and is currently pursuing her Doctorate of Philosophy in Organization and Management from Capella University.

Joy enjoys spending time with her children, singing and of course writing poetry. She has been writing for many years. This book includes poems that go back as far as when she was 9 years old.

Joy is a teacher to students of all ages (teaching various subjects including music) and currently she is an Instructor at various local colleges and colleges online. She gives seminars on public speaking, leadership, and other business related topics.

Joy's personal website…www.joylough.com will keep you up to date with other information. Stop by the site and leave a message!

Take Care

God Bless!

Joy Lough

Tears of Joy

Joy Lough

Tears of Joy

www.ingramcontent.com/pod-product-compliance
Lightning Source LLC
LaVergne TN
LVHW051842080426
835512LV00018B/3025